Dancing in the Light
A collection of poems

James Burkett

Living Hope Press
Ithaca, NY • 2018

Published by Living Hope Publishing
Ithaca, New York

Copyright 2018 by James Burkett
All rights reserved

Cover art by Kay Burkett

ISBN-10: 1719215200
ISBN-13 978 1719215206

Printed in the United States of America

for my good friends Bill and Jerry

who taught me it is OK to question
what we call sacred

Table of Contents

Finding Hope	10
Light in the Darkness	11
Beauty	12
That Which Brings Joy	13
God	14
God II	16
Beauty 2	18
Big Bang Theory	20
Beauty 3	22
The Light Within	23
That Required by God	24
Michael and Joseph, 1918	26
Uncertainty	28
Hope	28
Quaker Meditation Garden	29
pursuing the dance	31
Seeking the Essence	33
Quaker Meeting for Worship	34
Walk in the Light	35
Dancing in the Light	36
Joy 2	37
Hasten Unto God	38
Hunger	39
Light Shines Through Cracks	40
Original Sin	41
river of life	42
Unguarded	43
Don Quixote Meets the Mennonites	44
Merry Christmas	45
Prayer	46
Melodies from the Past	48
French Quarter	49
Christmas Prayer	50
Cliff	51

Acknowledgments

In January 2017 I resolved to write a poem each day. True to the resolution I ended the year with over 300 poems. Some poems were horrible, but others suggested possibility. From the poems several collections were compiled. The first, Dancing in the Light, was a collection that carried the influence of my Mennonite and Quaker background. My wife, Kay, read the collection and encouraged me to move forward with putting them into booklet form.

I was fortunate to become acquainted with Bruce Bennett, a retired professor in literature at Wells College in Aurora, New York. Bruce is a poet and agreed to read my collections of poetry. His feedback and tutoring proved to be extremely valuable. I learned much about the art of writing poetry from this master and can not thank him enough for his critique and suggestions. Without him this published collection would not have seen the sunlight.

Publishing a work, whether small or large is daunting. A casual conversation with Gerry Monaghan one Sunday evening led to his studio in Ithaca, New York where using his publishing background he began to pursue his dream of assisting people with small projects to publish their work. At his suggestion we pursued photo art taken by my wife Kay to include in the book. Gerry's work coalesced into the formation of Living Hope Publishing through which his design and lay out experience has made this collection beautiful. A final magnificent touch was to use a watercolor painting done by Kay Burkett as the cover art.

I am indebted to each of these people for their contributions for making Dancing in the Light a reality.

James Burkett
May 2018

Finding Hope

In the darkness there is light
In the cold there is warmth
In the chaos there is shalom
In the end there is a beginning

Light in the Darkness

We wallow in the long dark night
singing melodious songs
about a far away town
where bombs explode
and houses are bulldozed.

From the shadows a baby cries out
blinded by the clatter
of the "instruments of peace"
rumbling along their
silent path to shallow victory
enshrined forever in darkness.

Light gathers, spreading quietly
embodied in the soul of humanity,
a gift from the source of waters
casting out the night of bitterness.

Beauty

In the beginning was beauty.
Beauty lay over the face of infinity,
And the dazzling burst of light
That we call the Big Bang
Revealed the intense beauty
Of the universe
Calling us to love, and
Have compassion for all creation.

Now let it well up in your being
And spring forth in passion.
Are we not all children of the
Creator – human and beast alike
Each with a place
In that grand choir
Singing the boisterous song of breath?

Sing then out of the depths of the soul –
Not just a song of oneself,
But a concert of the unity of all life,
Of the beauty
    That surrounds,
That streams within and through
    All that is;
Of beauty created
And the beauty life creates.

That Which Brings Joy

When do I experience joy;
A state of great delight,
    Bliss,
        Serenity,
            Wonder, and
                Peace and calm within oneself?

Spending time with my wife
Spending time with my children
Spending time with my grandchildren
Visiting grandma on her farm
Delving into the genealogy
    Of our family
An infant grasping my finger
A small child falling asleep in my arms
Working at the food pantry
Volunteering at Lakewood Retreat

Writing poetry
Writing stories
Bird watching
Star gazing
Collecting stamps,
Inuit stone carvings, and
Native American pottery

God

When I was a child
He was a kindly old man
With gray hair and beard
Who lived in the sky.

When I was a teen
He was a strict parent
With unreasonable rules
Against which I rebelled.

When I was a young man
He was a wise mentor
With divine ideas and guidelines
That I strove to follow.

As I grew older
He became a leader
Pointing the way
For me to travel.

When I was middle age
She became a fierce warrior
Warring against injustice and evil
Protecting me from harm.

She played many roles
But I began to wonder
Who she really was
And what she really does.

No one seems able to comprehend them,
But everyone seeks them,
And most want to be in her presence
After their death.

Some claim to have talked with him.
Others see her
In epiphanic encounters.
Still we remain unable to name them.

God II

Defining God in anthropomorphic terms limits that which has no definition. God as an anthropomorphic being died. It really never existed except as a construct of human imagination.

Today I know God
as the ground of all existence
    as the source, energy force and essence of the universe
        as creativity
            as spirit – non material yet always present.

It is the creator of all that is;
in it all has life and being;
without it nothing that is would be;
it is ever present, creating a sense of awe,
beyond comprehension.
It always has been
and always will be.

Beauty 2

A baby's face,
The strength of a young wrestler,
The grace of a ballerina,
Figure skaters
Gliding across the ice,
Wrinkles on the face of an old woman,
The leathery face of an old man,
Salmon leaping the rapids,
The soaring eagle,
A fawn taking its first step,
The cheetah racing across the savannah,
A herd of caribou stretching
As far as the eye can see,
A blade of grass,
The newly budded flower,
A field of ripened wheat,
Whispering aspens,
Rugged forests,
The Amazon River,
Mountain streams tumbling
From lofty peaks,
Rainbows,

Sunsets,
Sailboats quietly slicing
Through the waters
Their sails billowing in the wind,
Michael Jordan doing a slam dunk,
Monks praying in the monastery,
Smoke from incense lifting to the heavens,
Prayer flags fluttering in the breeze,
Dirk Willems' hand reaching
For the one fallen through the ice,
Paintings and sculptures
By the masters,
Inuit soapstone and ivory carvings,
Pottery by Maria,
Furniture by Stickley,
Bring beauty and joy
Into our lives.

Big Bang Theory

In the beginning,
When was that?
The beginning!
The beginning of what?

The beginning of the world,
    Of the universe,
        Of everything.

Creativity always was.
No beginning?
No beginning – always was.

What about the big bang?
What was before that?
Creativity always was,
Declaring I will be, who I will be.

From whence did the stuff come
That exploded into our universe?

Creativity always was,
Nothing exists
Outside of Creativity.
Creativity exists in all universes –
    There is only one God.

All universes, there is more than one?
Space extends forever.
What is beyond our universe?
What was before our universe?

Life blossoms.
Life ceases.
Stars burn brightly.
Stars burn out.
The universe expands.
The universe collapses into oblivion.

Matter and energy
Dance in Creativity
Forever cycling.
A mystery!

From whence you come
Thereto shall you return.

Beauty 3

Beauty surrounds all;
It is within all.
Remove the scabs
From your eyes.
Behold!
Once disdainful,
The sludge of life
From a new perspective
Shimmers in radiance.

Did not God offer
Redemption to all?

The Light Within

Acts of kindness,
Friendly gestures,
Helping others,
Sharing resources
Of self and time and money
Come to me without a thought;
But it's mighty difficult
    To acknowledge
        And to see
"That of God"
    Abides in me.

That Required by God

Be humble.
Mourn for tragedy.
Be meek.
Seek (restorative/distributive) justice.
Be merciful/compassionate/loving.
Be pure.
Be a peacemaker.
Be an example.
Do not put others down.
Be reconciled.
Treat others with respect.
Be truthful.
Turn the other cheek/do not retaliate.
Absorb violence.
Share your possessions.
Love your enemies.
Give to the needy.
Pray quietly.
Forgive others.
Do not worry.
Seek the kingdom.
Do not judge others.
Do to others what you would have them do to you.
Ask for blessings.
Be patient.
Be hospitable.
Be joyful.
Love God.
Love your neighbor.

Michael and Joseph, 1918

Michael and Joseph Hofer, brothers from a Hutterite colony in South Dakota, were drafted into the U.S. Army in 1917. As conscientious objectors they refused to wear the army uniform and participate in military exercises. They were court-martialed and sentenced to Alcatraz where they suffered from torture, cold damp conditions, and lack of food. In 1918 they were transferred to Ft. Leavenworth prison in a weakened and dire condition. Shortly thereafter, they died.

Michael hung
from his hands, chained to bars
above his head.
Brother Joseph hung
beside him.
Couldn't even swat
the menacing mosquitoes
lunching in the damp,
cold, dark prison cell.

They hung there
with little to eat
and little to wear;
often beaten
for their refusal
to wear the military uniform
and participate
in the war effort.

When the breath
became too raspy,
and the lungs
rattled loudly
their forms lay
on cold hard beds,
beyond resuscitation
waiting for their loved ones
to come and bid goodbye.

Death took them
because they refused
    to kill.

When the wives
at last arrived
they beheld these
gallant brothers
bedecked in cursed uniform
lying in wooden boxes.

Retrieving them into their care,
they dressed them in humble attire, and
buried them in the cold damp earth,
martyrs in the quest for peace.

Uncertainty

Life yells two constants
Unwaning impermanence
And uncertainty

Hope

Cruising my brain streets
Where does hope abide in me?
It springs from my heart.

Quaker Meditation Garden

Approach the garden
Amidst the blooming flowers
Find restful repose

Peaceful garden
Listen to the sounds of nature
Jet flies overhead

Gentle garden site
Assailed by modern rumble
Yet there is bird song

Garden of nature
Surrounded by pollution
Absorb our carbon

Amicable garden
Encompassed by the fast-paced life
Teach creation care

How we imagine God
informs the central
dynamic of our lives.

pursuing the dance

"where your treasure is stored up
there also is your heart"

our fathers and mothers
the peace lovers
the rebaptizers
those fervent for the gospel
followers of jesus
martyred, exiled
refugees in a foreign wilderness

no longer remembered
by a generation eager
to marry the dove
and the eagle
pursuing a golden bull

deluded into thinking
the way is clear
through religious clubs
of qualified love
and exclusive membership
that allows the chosen
to reside with god forever
in an afterlife of glory

yet searching for the fire
that ignites the soul
to leave all that's earthly behind
and dance with god

Beyond good and evil
there is a space where
we must meet.

Seeking the Essence

Is love the essence?
No,
Though of
    faith,
        hope,
            and love,
love is the greatest.

What then is essential?
Seeking the spirit of the divine!
Love is a byproduct.

Quaker Meeting for Worship

We sit in silence
And await
Listening expectantly
For God to speak;
For sudden peal of thunder,
And the rushing wind
Of the first century,
For tongues of fire
And tongues unintelligible,
For magic from the sky.

Today the only rushing wind –
A monstrous furnace
Generously limbed.
Through its arteries hot air blows,
But no tongues of fire
On the gathered doth it bestow.
The only human sound
Slight rustling, occasional coughing
And silence all around.

Where is the mighty God of yore,
The one who through old Israel tore?
God is with us yet today,
Understood a different way;
No longer the old man in the sky,
But the presence always nigh
That doth whisper in your ear
If you sit and wait to hear.

Walk in the Light

We hover restlessly
Striving and bending
Toward the incomprehensible light
Seeking to pierce the veil

Like insects
Attracted in the night
To the glow of light
They pound against the screen

Seeking an opening
To allow
Flight to the source
And oblivion

The light is the path
Not the destination

Dancing in the Light

Words by Hafiz the poet:
"Every child knows God;
Not the god of names,
Not the god of dos and don'ts,
Not the god of weird things,
But the God who says,
'Come dance with me.'"

When did we begin
To decline the invitation?
When did we decide
To dance on our own –
Some call that
Dancing with the devil?

Still we yearn to "dance with God."
But it doesn't happen in religion;
It doesn't happen in correct doctrine;
It doesn't happen in piety,
Or a myriad of other practices
Ascribed to the divine.

How then –
Dance in truth;
Dance in mercy;
Dance in humility;
Dance in hope;
Dance in faith;
Dance in love;
And above all come –
Dance in the glory of the light.

Joy 2

Joy is found
In magical places –
   The farm on a clear,
      Moonless,
         Starlit,
            Summer night
The shores of Hudson Bay
   In late autumn
      Watching polar bears
      Await the ice
         Under the northern lights
Among the ruins of Machu Pichu
   Sitting alone on the ground
      Within the stone walls of a restored home
         Feeling the energy of life gone before
Standing on the Great Wall
   Looking into the distance
      And seeing it wind over mountains
      And through valleys
Standing in the Sequoia forest
   Looking up at massive trees
      Growing to the heavens
Seeing the Rocky Mountains
   In the distance
      From the high plains
         And thinking they are a bank of clouds
Sitting in the bombed out Catholic Church
   In a small village
      In the mountains of El Salvador
         Listening to the priest discuss accompaniment

Hasten Unto God

I am appalled by inhumanity to others.
I am appalled by disregard for environmental conditions.
I am appalled by the immense injustice perpetrated on others.
I am appalled by my indifference.
What then shall be done?

Hasten unto God.
Align with Love.
Keep your heart open.
Practice mindfulness.
Pray without ceasing.
Fast
Study the way.
Live simply.
Practice solitude.
Serve others.
Confess shortcomings.
Worship your God.
Seek the Light.
Celebrate.

Choose love.
Distain hatred.
Do justice.
Be slow to judge.
Walk humbly.
Be a point of light.

Hunger

Sometimes I wonder
What it must be like to be hungry
I mean – really hungry
Like not having enough food
Like the little man scraping
The inside of your stomach
Like the dog gnawing
On your tongue
Trying to find a flavor
Like the senses graying
And the lights growing dim

Orchards are blooming
The harvest ripens
Surplus rots in the fields
Granaries overflow
Plenty abounds
In the midst of poverty
And hunger

The grip of power
Steals from the widow
The machine of economy
Grinds the orphan
Distributive justice denied
Tonight he goes to bed
With nothing to eat

Feed the hungry
Give drink to the thirsty
The work thereof
The work of God

Light Shines Through Cracks

Maybe I can't see
The light within me
Because I've willed
To keep the cracks filled

Maybe I'm blind
Deeds that are kind
Emit a light
Not hidden from sight

Original Sin

Cain raised his hand against Abel.
The world held its breath.
Original sin so shameful
one must hide from God.

How to keep the violence in check?
Eve's story – more beguiling –
shifts the focus
from violence to sex.

Blame a woman.
No longer a need
to contain the violence
now construed as redemptive.

Talons of the eagle
grip with awe.
Power tantalizes the imagination
of peace through victory.

Bow, worship the violence
wrought by Aquila.

The dove weeps.

river of life

river of time
we journey with you
through swirling eddies
and meandering channels
we cross deep pools
navigate swift rapids
carried in the current
of changing seasons
reaching the ocean of oneness
to be lifted to the clouds
and dropped
at the headwaters
to journey again
the river of life

Unguarded

Sometimes thoughts
Of militant domination
Momentarily flood my soul,
And I become convinced
That victory brings peace.

The thoughts cause me to shutter.
The idea, out of sync
With my ardent pacifism,
Come when I am unguarded
Against the evil that can overwhelm

Don Quixote Meets the Mennonites

Take counsel gallant one
With pious community
Mouth of the heart
Spew thy passions
Incoherent yet sagacious
For discernment by elders
Let them chew
As a dog with plastic bone
Gnaws forever
And never consumes
Engage Plato
With Rumi
Tilt at the windmills
Of your blessed society
For you know in your heart
As you lay bleeding
Your battle wounds will be bound
By that fervent assembly

Merry Christmas

Hark ye, and lend an ear.
Some say it's a time of cheer
Others find the season drear

Merchants look to profiteer
In the gay atmosphere

New merchandise doth domineer
And in the windows fast appear

Everywhere you turn you hear
Music from a balladeer

Writ to calm our inmost fear
And to a righteous way adhere

Therefore, abandon all the season schmear
Commercializing to the rear

'Cause in the eye there's a tear
Life is so much more austere

Many wear a thin veneer
Suffering from events severe

Attitudes of joy and cheer
Seem to some so cavalier

A word, a deed done sincere
Helps us all to persevere

With compassion, spread and smear
Love throughout the whole sphere

Herein you can pioneer
Upon uncharted wild frontier

Making it your sole career
To see the light and spread the cheer

Prayer

The world over
    People pray,
For blessings for themselves
For blessings for others
For healing for themselves
For healing for others
For forgiveness
For direction
For favors
For escape
For peace
For relief from anxiety.
    And people pray
Thanksgiving
Joy
And elation.

People pray to their gods:
Some in deep supplication
Some with tears
Some with anger
And other strong emotions.
Still others pray to their gods
With casual superficiality.
Some expect answers.
Others are not sure.

People pray to gods that are
Superhuman candy men (or women)
Anthropomorphic creatures
Existing in space somewhere,
Giving and taking

Intervening or laissez-faire
Depending on their moods, whims,
    How impressed they are
With the manner in which the humans pray.

Some people use
    Candles
        Incense
            And other medium
In sending their words of praise and supplication
To the holy presence of the world.

A few people pray with intensity,
Uttering the deep murmurs and sighs
Of their inner soul;
Never expecting an answer to prayer,
Simply content to join
The spirit force of the universe.

Melodies from the Past

Sung a Cappella
In four-part harmony
Drift through my mind
And burst from the closed spaces
Of church sanctuary

Warbled to the rhythm
Of water splashing
Over head and body
Standing naked before God
In daily baptismal ritual

Fanny Crosby's hymns
Belted out with exuberant
Evangelical joy

"Blessed assurance, Jesus is mine"
"The vilest offender…"
Must be me
"Who truly believes"
"Love unbounded hides…
In the cleft of the rock"
Where is the rock?

"To God be the glory"
I am an "heir of salvation"
"Tell of His excellent greatness"
I should sing all day long
'Cause I've nothing else to do
"But rise in the arms of faith"

"This is my story, this is my song"
"Draw me nearer, nearer"
To the blood pouring
From His speared side
As "angels descend…
And whisper love"

French Quarter

In the French Quarter
Debauchery and madness
God is very near

Beggars in the street
Children of the Holy One
Teaching us to share

Jazz musicians,
Pulsating rhythms
Reverberating from heaven

Flowing spirits
River of humanity
God's children – Bourbon Street

Christmas Prayer

Go boldly.
Look for the light in humankind.
Bring peace with your presence.
Serve others,
Especially –
The poor
    The hungry
        The sick
            The refugee/immigrant
                And those who are marginalized.

For in serving others
You serve the divine.
And in that service
You enter holy space.
You come into
    The presence of God
        And truly celebrate Christmas.

Cliff

A cliff looms ahead
And you may have to jump off.
Grow wings as you fall.

Plunging into the abyss
Ascend to challenges
With wings of strength.

About the Author

James Burkett spent his career working with emotionally and behaviorally challenged children and their families. After retiring he moved with his wife to the Finger Lakes region in New York to be near grandchildren. He loves summer when he can go barefooted and wears sandals when footwear is required. He also loves to travel and has traveled to all of the states in the United States except Alaska. And he hopes to travel there in the future.

Made in the USA
Lexington, KY
20 September 2018